A BOOK OF POETRY

LEAVES CLAPPING

JAN MARQUART

ISBN: 978-1-7324983-9-6

Produced by Publish Pros | publishpros.com

OTHER BOOKS BY JAN MARQUART

Write to Heal
The Mindful Writer, Still the Mind, Free the Pen
The Basket Weaver, a Novel
Kate's Way, a Novel
Echoes from the Womb, a Book for Daughters
Voices from the Land
The Breath of Dawn, a Journey of Everyday Blessings
How to Write from Your Heart (booklet)
How to Write Your Own Memoir (booklet)
A Manual on How to Deal with a Bully in the Workplace
A Writer's Wisdom
Unveil the Wounded Self, a Guided Journal for PTSD Sufferers
Never Too Late, a Novel
Cracked Open, a Book of Poems
Light, a Book of Poems
Eternal, a Book of Poems
Still, a Book of Haiku

CHILDREN'S BOOKS

Can You Find My Love? (Book series also available in Spanish)

Book 1: Seasons   *Book 6: Bugs*
Book 2: Things to Do Outside   *Book 7: In the Sea*
Book 3: Why We Need Rain   *Book 8: Morning*
Book 4: Things with Wheels   *Book 9: On Your Head*
Book 5: Families (English only) *Book 10: Babies*

Poetry is nearer to vital truth than history.

PLATO

ACKNOWLEDGMENTS

Jimmy Santiago Baca, you are an inspirational overcomer. The tough questions you taught me to ask of my writing kept me going forward. You ride the soul's journey with your students. Thank you for an amazing journey.

Judyth Hill, you are graceful and encouraging, a mentor and extraordinary poet. Working with you was simply delicious.

Rich Carnahan and Mary Hall at Publish Pros, your grace, respect, inspiration, and care for my work over the years has established a relationship of faithfulness and trust. To a writer, that means everything.

Susan Hutchinson and Scott Hastie, your comments, suggestions, and honesty were invaluable.

Mom, your creativity always had me in awe—the way you came up with ideas, poems, and projects placed a seed inside me to find that part of myself—I am forever inspired by you. I acknowledge you and dedicate this book to you. When I write, you are always beside me.

To all, a huge resounding THANK YOU!

RESOURCES

Ghazal created by Abdullah Jafar Rudaki, the first canonical ghazal writer of Persia circa ninth century. Page 3

Pillow Book. Sei Shōnagon, circa 966-1025, Japan; written in zuihitsu style. Page 36

All words in italic were extracted from "To Go To Lvov." Adam Zagajewski, translated by Renata Gorczynski, and put in its own piece. Page 46

CONTENTS

WILD SPIRITS

WILD SOULS

Whether we commune with wild spirits in the quick leap of a squirrel, the soul of an ancestor, or the stories of our lives, the leaves will be clapping in celebration.

Leaves clapped in the wind. I looked around
wondering why the applause.

Oh, I remembered.

It's Fall.

WILD SPIRITS

FOR SUCH A TIME AS THIS

Hard red earth held me up.
I once had a vision of such a time as this.

Ancient pinions surrounded my home.
They waited for me for such a time as this.

Desert silence gently held me together.
Its strength was meant for such a time as this.

Howling winds whipped protection around my land.
Its message aligned for such a time as this.

Jan, human life has shallow roots.
The Universe's root is love for such a time as this.

GIFTS FROM GOD?

Apples cooked to the
texture of flannel
one dash of cinnamon
one pinch of cloves
the scent wafting
through the rooms.

I throw the naked cores
into the barren yard
for the fluffy-tailed squirrels.

Eager
they jump over my weathered
fence, bite them the way a
cat holds her kittens
in her teeth and
carry them
to mysterious destinations
back over the wooden fence
tails flicking in delight.

They don't look back as I
Call out Enjoy!
My cotton dishtowel draped
over my shoulder to wipe apple
juice from my
hands.

I wonder—
Do they think I am God
giving them a miracle?

Isn't it all so delicious?

SHOULD HAVE

underneath powdered snow
a pale tangle of decaying dry weeds
meant to be burned
lost its tomorrows
with fallen leaves.

THE UNKNOWN ARTIST

I watched the artist weave
fragments of dried leaves
stems from a catnip bush
strings fallen after garbage pickups
items anyone in their right mind thought was trash
until her task was done.

To the artist
these items were invaluable
weaving them daily
until her task was done.

She favored mud clods
fallen pine needles
small pieces of plastic
and kept weaving
until her task was done.

Ne'er a single complaint was heard
her task still undone.

The time came
when skinless heads
poked against delicate shells
and reached for the sky
her task still undone.

The artist searched for
wriggling worms
tiny flies
unknown delicacies
until her task was done.

The father sat nearby
a watch of protection
as any good father would do
until his task was done.

One day, like all children,
they flew away
as did their mother, the artist,
and their father, the protector,
their tasks now done.

A ladder under my feet
I climbed high
studied the intricate
home she wove
until her task was done.

Tears filled my eyes
touched by the perfection
of the sturdy miniature abode
her task now done.

A small unknown artist
wove a masterpiece
and I didn't even
get her name.

But watched until
her task was
done.

THE OTHER HALF

The silver moon sliced
into the late-night sky
only a grey shadow for
its other half
caught me off-guard
while in pure solitude.

In reverence
I stared into her hidden self
my eyes penetrating
the unexposed body
wishing for her full goddess self.

It is there, her missing other,
it is there.

But it is absent now and I am sad.
I refuse to believe she is half gone.
I remember the nights I saw her
in completeness—her radiant glow
melting into ocean waves
laying over dry fields
emboldening my window.

Oh, full moon
don't hide yourself from me.

I have suffered enough grief.

YOU & ME

A robust storm hit my windows
awakening me at 3:08 am.
An ungodly hour for any human to be awake.

Frustrated, I arose to busy myself,
cleaned out the fridge,
looked for misplaced things,
read Robert Hass
Mary Oliver
the book of Genesis.

Great eagle, I think, we are each driven
to rise higher
reach towards God
to survive the
turbulence of dark storms.

We have overcome,
you and me,
the ordeals of
transformation.

SURPRISES

jaded by life's challenges
I escaped to the desert
and found a foreign world
that startled me back to life

cacti blossoms radiantly showed off hot pink blossoms
yucca plants stood erect their waxy white bells bowing
Mexican hat wildflowers red and yellow intertwined
with buffalo grass

drunken crickets the color of granny smith apples
walked sideways
miniature ancient pinion trees dotted the land
purple sage plants spread wide
mountains changed colors at dusk

ant hills mounded in raised piles
spiders varied in stripes, spots, and hues the size of
golf balls as long as a stick of chewing gum

snakes dressed in geometric patterns some
red, thin as a pencil fast as a train
some wearing skins of green lazily slithered for a day's
walk
road runners dragged their long tails barely touching
ground

quail led a trail of teeny babies showing off new families
bunnies born from shallow holes cautiously climbed to
ground
jack rabbits leapt across the land the size of dogs
horny toad lizards walked into the sun out of mud huts
others canary yellow and baby blue raced under bushes

bumble bees the size of chicken eggs fed on lobelia
bushes
coyotes sang in the dark to those miles away
moths like sage green lace decorated walls in the sun
or were dark grey as big as shoes with one large orange
dot on pure white under wings

tumbleweeds sped with alacrity as if being chased by
demons
winds whipped adobe walls howling

triple rainbows followed vibrant storms wide and
hopeful
iridescent ravens cleaned up dead things
sky at dusk brilliant in purple, orange, yellow, pink,
green, and blue welcomed the night

silent whisperings of God omnipresent to those who
listened
space

lots of space

QUESTION

Does rain regret flooding?
Does heat regret singeing grass?
Does wind regret knocking over a tree?

I rescued a moth from battering itself against my
window. I cupped my hands around
its delicate wings tickling my palms.

Joyfully, I opened the door and uncupped my hands
sending its tiny self into flight
to enjoy the sunny Santa Fe air.

Just as the moth spread its wings
an average-looking bird
swooped down
caught the moth in its beak
and flew away.

I let out a scream.
No!

I had intended to rescue the small delicate moth
but sent it to its death instead.

Should I regret the death of the moth
or smile, knowing I fed a bird its morning manna?

TRADE-OFF

on the way back from the beach
the sand warm as a heating blanket
I stopped by an acre of acacia trees
to snap off three large sprigs of
canary yellow flowers
the sun resting inside each bud

radiant, pungent, fragrant
I placed them in a large mason jar
put them in the middle of my table
such delicious angel grace

but one day I walked to the grove
to get more blossoms
and saw a group of men with bulldozers razing them
with fury to build a noisy smelly bar
where people get drunk
speak of meaningless things
as those intoxicated are likely to do
gorging themselves on greasy fries and lousy food

Is this the best man can do?

SONG OF THE CRICKETS

Aunt Mabel lived
behind fields wide and spacious
where there was no dearth of crickets
to keep me awake at night.

Oh, how I hated those crickets.

Now that I am older
I open my window at night
and sleep better to the songs of the crickets
their hind legs rubbing
with symphonic delight.

They need no men in black suits to
frantically wave a baton
don't have to practice till midnight
or worry about mistakes in their performances.

In the city streets
I watch gardeners spray poison
they tell me they want to get rid of the
crickets because people don't like them
and are afraid those pests will get in their houses.

Only to sing, I shout,
        only to
                sing!

STORMS

It is sunset.

A storm births.

Blades of sharp light puncture the earth
saturating winds with scents of
dust, hay, cacti blossoms.

The sky screams in agony or
maybe those hollering sounds
are simply those of delight.

It is difficult to tell
as wind picks up everything in its path
purging the wanted and unwanted
breaking glass
removing trees
making everyone rush out of its way.

What a mess!

I ask the wind
haven't I had enough storms to clean up after?

A dark cloud shoots flashes of light,
winking.

I will pass

I assure you.

I always do. Keep going!

MOUNTAINS

Even a mountain
can be brought down by
a storm.

I've seen mountains
big
strong
mighty.

I've climbed mountains
steep
rocky
steadfast.

I've overcome mountains
obstructive
blocking
overwhelming.

I've witnessed mountains
slide down to the ground
kill, smother, drown
all in its way.

Oh, the great mountains whose only fear is
the tiny mustard seed.

PEACE

The milky sky
looks tired as if the
sun stole its color.

A young red squirrel
perched on my fence stares into
the muted sky.

Sits, oh so still
as if not breathing
then abruptly leaps
to a leafless branch
jutting out from the Crone tree.

Hands around a warm
cup of tea
I witnessed the
soundless jump.

The sky and I --
in peace.

MOON

I asked the new moon,
where have you hidden
your other part?

It answered back,
where do you keep your secrets?
Do you put them in the light for all to see, or, like me,
find a place, a sacred place, and hide them there?

Moon, I asked, a few weeks ago you showed all of you,
what did you do with your secrets then?

The same as you, it said,

I'm good at pretending too.

TRUTH OR FICTION

An airplane marks the unscarred sky with
streaks of white.

isn't it the air that is being marked
but what is the air
we say it is the sky, but how do we know

do we even have a sky

is there such a thing

does the sky have a front or back
side or bottom

or is the concept of sky only a name
we give nothing

How can it be that we use words to describe nothing
while everyone knows we mean something?

LANGUAGE OF SILENCE

quiet breathing
softly finds its rhythm
its motion a gentle slide
in and out
out and in

prayers
reach God
not a moment
too soon
in deep rest

breezes
sweetly kiss
the lotus blossom
emboldened by pink and white clouds above
softening

snowflakes
cool as a wave
restful as meditation
delicious as a smile

The sound of silence
Is the language of God.

The sound of silence
Is the language of God.

S K Y

Sky, I watch you as blue melts into creamy white like
the film over the old lady's nut-brown eyes.

I have too many questions and Carl Sagan is dead.
Is he beyond the milky sky?
Is that where everyone goes when they die?

Lost in curiosity. No one these days seems to know,
really know, a damn thing. Everyone is guessing, and
thinking, and suspecting.

I stare at you, lost in thought.

Sky, you look like egg whites that aren't quite cooked
enough.

If I crack you open, what will drop out upon me?

THE MESSAGE

the Crone is draped in golden light
vibrant green leaves
a shawl over her twisted limbs
have dressed her for the season
ready to attend a delightful
gala where she will arrive well-dressed

in obvious glory
her radiance shoots
from her like
flashes of fire
brightening the night

I do not know what kind of tree she is
her body so ordinary brown
her branches slightly bent with
the heaviness of aged wisdom
her grace hidden in the wrinkles
of her bark

branches and vines from
other trees
hug her close
like children once lost but now
reunited with a mother

hundreds of juniper trees stand
behind her
strong and tall
waving in the mild wind
like bridesmaids milling about

MY AFFAIR

Oversized calla lilies
grow in a row against my rented Victorian
dense, sweet, earthy
like rebirthing.

In the early morning
I sew
write
study
cook
my lover unattending like a pair of old socks in my
wicker basket.

Pruners in hand I cut a dozen calla lilies
put them in a vase
their soft yellow powder falls on my palm
softening my arid hands.

My lover still ensconced in only himself.

The sensuous, scented powder
a secret reminder
that God put love in the calla lily.

My refuge.

My secret love.

WILD SOULS

*A poet looks at the world the way
a man looks at a woman.*

WALLACE STEVENS

I AM

I am the hem that is too revealing.
I am shrimp sauteing in aromatic olive oil.
I am a child's bike pedal squealing in delight.
I am Wagner making music out of Tristan and Isolde's
    tragedy.
I am the semi-colon breaking my life into two wholes.
I am light shining on darkness.
I am cold water refreshing dry hearts.
I am the red of the perky robin.
I am the hoot of the baby owl singing into still nights.
I am the flute filling tunnels with spirituality.
I am Persephone changed into a new destiny.
I am the syllables of Thursday.
I am Alice dropping into deep holes.
I am the triangle seeing three directions.
I am the vivid red of a Latina's passion.
I am waves streaked by the full moon.
I am the golden nectar of a daylily.

TO KEEP A MAN — OR NOT

I was told I needed a strong man
one with broad shoulders
one who knew how to handle a woman's ambition
no doubt, I have strong ambition.

I was told I needed someone who could make his world
big enough for me
In order to have enough room to move about
make my soups
write my books
sew my dresses
have lots of friends
decorate my home
sit in nature
study new things.

I like myself, I said. I have worked hard to become the
woman I desired to be.

No, he said, I needed to sacrifice a part of myself to
keep a man.

Really, I asked?

And just what part of me should that be?

PRISM OF MOURNING

I cry
   because that is what any sane person would do.

I cry for the loss of my father's voice; it was the
   feeling of home.
I cry for the loss of my mother; she was my connection
   to strength.
I cry for the loss of my Nana whose hugs taught my
   heart fullness.
I cry for the loss of my family. I am now an orphan.

I grieve
   because that is what any sane person would do.

I grieve for families in Ukraine suffering the
   unimaginable.
I grieve for the innocent people in prison.
I grieve for those sleeping on sidewalks all over the
   world.
I grieve for men who kill too easily because they do not
   know the effort in the creation of childbirth.

I lament
   because that is what any sane person would do.

I lament because some poets choose whispers for voices.
I lament because another dear friend has died, and I
   couldn't help her.
I lament because there are life-defying diseases and
   people are dying.
I lament because war is not the answer to peace.

I sob
        because that is what any sane person would do.

I sob because my accomplishments are misunderstood
                for the harvests of hard times that they are.
I sob because challenges are endless.
I sob because hearts are failing to endure.
I sob because life is too big to hold still.

I sweetly weep
        because that is what any sane person would do.

I sweetly weep because a small bird sung me awake
              with a delicate song.
I sweetly weep because I found the right word for a new
              poem.
I sweetly weep because I found hope today.
I sweetly weep because love can never be destroyed.

LOVE LETTERS TO TEAS

I love your aroma, Russian Caravan
you are deep and pungent
seducing me into your rich forest
into your deep heart which
opens like the sky after rain
your fertile soil heartily kissing
me as my lips come near

and you tender-leafed Green
you are light as a fairy
with your tenderness
allowing me to drift in a dream
until I awaken
you are as joyous as a bird's song
first thing in the morning

and what about you Oolong
oh, rich robust Oolong
your taste is like that of spicey foods
from foreign places
you fill my breath with the flavor of
wisdom and grace
you are my warm blanket
on cold, rainy days

but wait, what about you oh delicate Jasmine
you with your goddess fragrance from tiny flowers that
join me in mornings when I
pick up my pen to write
you are like a mother's love
staying wide with the horizon of the page
allowing me to be free
your spirit's touch

your delicate kisses
keep me company
as new poems spring forth

See you tomorrow.

TELL ME

A rill of tears shed
diurnally as mourners stand
at gravestones
flowers limp in their hands
some so fresh their
aromas lift
the heavy air
of grief.

Wishes for times past
are left at stones
if only we could live
one more hour of those
moments we didn't see then
were so deeply
engraved with
love.

What is it about life
that what we didn't want then
seems the answer for today?

GO AHEAD—I DARE YOU!

Go ahead and fail
Fail big.

Go ahead and succeed
Succeed big.

Put it out there –
Fly or fall.

Go ahead.
Make your move, whatever it is.

Give it all you've got.

Swallow the trials of life.
Burn in the fire!
Rise again –
Go ahead.

I dare you!

PILLOW NOTES

Things that bring forth the Divine

> sitting in a Basilica
> praying in the woods
> stained-glass windows
> soup made with pungent spices
> a coo from a child
> a smile from an old man sitting in the sun
> the smell of lilac
> vibrant pink cactus blossoms

Rare Things

> friends uninhibited to cry with you
> men who talk about their emotions
> finding a four-leaf clover
> flowers received for no reason

Fond Memories

> pistachio ice cream with dad on hot August
> nights
> late-night swims at Coney Island with dad and
> Uncle Harold
> bowling with mom
> Nana's rice pudding and lemon meringue pie
> great grandma teaching me how to remove the
> skin without cutting off any of the
> potato
> Grandma making lemonade with white sugar
> Poppy giving me a book about flowers, his
> copper pennies and silver spoons
> finding the right lipstick color

discovering blood on my underwear and mom
telling me I had become a woman
hugging my favorite redwood tree at Nicene Marks

Things that sing in the dark

activated faith
a prayer of praise
a phone's ring
a new dream birthing
birds

Things that have lost their power

ex-boyfriends
my mother's anger
my sister's condemnation
blame for the emotions of others
desire to be married

LACEY

I have rainbows
coming out of
my fingers, she said.

Her man left her
and her baby for
another woman
who wound up leaving him
for peace.

I have rainbows
coming out of
my fingers, she said.

And began to decorate
her home
anchoring herself
to her own heart
each room a vivid theme
rebirthing her love of life.

She painted with beloved colors
filled vases with roses
draped flowers over wrought iron bedposts
and smiled.

Every woman needs a home
to remind her of who she is.

I have rainbows
coming out of
my fingers, she said.

Her smile as bright
as the moon.

CRONE

She stands in regal position
her trunk solid and ancient
thick branches spread wide—reaching.

                                 At 5, my mother told me my
father wanted a boy.

The long vines and misshaped trees majestically adorn the Crone
covering her identity as they spread out over her old body and
gnarled limbs snuggling close.

                                 At 12, my mother told me I
wasn't wanted—she had loved working in the world.

Crone faces me through my study window, watching
I smile at her, my heart calming, I am accepted
for all that I am.

                                 At 22, my mother told me my
dream should be to please her and have kids. I loved my mother.
Could I really not be enough?

Squirrels in arboreal locomotion race across
her knotted limbs
squealing in a giggle of play
cardinals, bluebirds, sparrows nestle in her vibrant foliage chirping
people awake.

What does the Crone do with all this responsibility?
she grows taller
she grows stronger
welcoming, always welcoming.

                                                     JAN MARQUART

At 34, I lost my mother. I failed
her. I am a barren woman with two college degrees.

This is what poets write about:
unrequited love.

Crone's persistent reaching awakens my longing
to have a place called home
inside the embrace
of a mother.

I tell you
the Crone is calling –

Come to me!

Come to me!

HELLO, IN CASE YOU WANT
TO KNOW ABOUT ME

I am a tigress. You cannot tame me.

When I can't sleep, I make a pot of soup or sometimes a
cheesy casserole.

I like watching the moon melt on the ocean.

I read poetry and lots of it.

I perseverate over the placement of vases on a shelf
striving for the most beautiful arrangement.
I love beauty.

I have different flavors of toothpaste to use
intermittently. I dance to the song of abundance.

I throw out the white of a hardboiled egg because it is
rubbery and tasteless.

I read four books at a time.

I write three books at a time.

I write every day. I won't tell you what I write, why I
write, or let you read it, unless my mood changes.

I wear natural fiber clothing to feel connected to the
earth.

I am self-disciplined.

I love lilies. Feel free to buy them for me, anytime, you

don't need an occasion.

I do not eat in bed. Food and sleep are divinely separate.

Friendship is my most treasured relationship.

If I don't matter to you find someone else to play with.

Write me something. I'll keep it forever. Break my heart, I'll burn it in my hibachi.

I watch movies I like over and over again. Have you seen The Philadelphia Story twenty times?

The handmade pens on my desk connect to my soul. I don't let anyone use them. So don't use one.

I need my kitchen clean. If you make a mess cooking, clean up or the mess will be put in your shoes or coat pocket.

I don't like anyone using my towel or toothbrush.

My mornings start out with prayers to God.

My evenings end with prayers to God.

I love generosity.

I enjoy making wishes on stars.

I gravitate towards people who believe in something bigger than themselves.

I hug old trees.

I love the sound of rain, the smell of home cooking, and the warmth of a hug.

I like heated sand on my feet.

Soft colors are my favorites except red, I like hot red.

I am tenacious, I cry easily, I laugh—a lot.

You might make an impact on me, but you cannot tell me who I am.

I bow to birds and butterflies.

Now, tell me about you.

LESSONS LEARNED

I have learned to sit in silence.
I have learned to still my mind.
I have learned to shut my mouth.
I have learned to listen to the birds chirping, the soup
  bubbling, the wind moving my clothes drying over
  the fence.
I have learned to feel the beat of my heart.
I have learned to watch my thoughts without
  condemnation.
I have learned to acknowledge when I don't know the
  answer.
I have learned to sit with my pen and be okay if it
  doesn't move.
I have learned to sit with my ghosts and other things I
  don't like.
I have learned the empty page is an opportunity.
I have learned to pray deeply.

I have learned life can't be controlled.

RESURRECTION

To leave in haste
is to forget many things
and sets your nervous system
to need recalibration.

The Basilica on the corner has
its *gardens* and trees
pruned as if the
world is perfect.

Holiday *wreaths*
are welcome mats
on the Basilica's huge wooden doors
and suddenly just as you
get to the door tired of running
you remember your lover's gift
of *Queen Anne cherries*
you hid in the last drawer of your great-grandmother's
bureau
so your mother won't
find them because you know
if she does she will eat them all
and you genuflect
in prayer
for their survival.

The Basilica is
a *breathless* sight
on the day of Christ's birth
and the *bells* have *pealed*
for the last half hour
encores of echoes that have
vibrated the air around it into

Holy prayer resurrecting
every soul
within a mile to bow.

Frenzy in the air falls
to its knee in susurrations
as fragile as China *teapots*
while in the distance
bullet trains are being born.

DON'T HATE MY NANA

Nana loved color
no tans, beiges, blacks, or grey colors for her
flaming red was the spirit of her soul
she was told to tone it down
she was in America now

her soft dresses let her full body flow
she had no desire to be skinny like Twiggy
her full hips swayed to their own rhythm
no tailored pants or jeans to squeeze
or hide her body
no puffy dos teased to frame her face

her lips were smoothed with bright red lipstick
no childish pinks, oranges, or burnt browns for this Puerto Rican
woman
she enjoyed her rice and beans with everything
made pies from scratch, no Betty Crocker for her

Nana had her ways.
She didn't want our ways.

Nana knew food secrets not even the doctors knew
laughter was the best medicine, she said, then made me
laugh
she didn't believe in underwear
elastic garters like large rubber bands held up her
stockings worn up to her thighs
no high heels for my Nana
she liked her feet touching the ground and preferred
my father's old corduroy slippers because they were comfortable

Nana was her own woman.
Well, who else should she be?

HISTORY

Wind bites rocks and they take it.
Darkness swallows day and it takes it.
The full moon as witness.

Life slaps at me.
I'm not as strong as the rock or the day.
The moon as my witness.
Some challenges seem
unmanageable.

Nana, I wonder, at 16
in the early 1900s
how did you manage after arriving at Ellis Island
knowing no English
not being able to read or write?

How did you manage?

Grandma, I wonder, at 29
in the 1920s
how did you manage
the betrayal of the father of your
two children
one still in the womb while
raising your
four nieces and nephews as well?

How did you manage?

Great grandma, I wonder, at 18
in the late 1880s
how did you manage
married life at only 18

cooking for 18 farms hands?

How did you manage?

Mom, I wonder, at 18
in the early 1940s
how did you manage
the oppression of women
that stole your dream to
become a scientist?

How did you manage?

Photos of these strong women sit
on a table near my bed
reminding me that I too
can manage
a diagnosis of cancer.

All of you,
you are my mountains of strength
breathing in my blood.

You can do it
You can do anything, I hear them chant.

You are us.

We are you!

You can manage!

MY MOTHER'S SCREAMS

I was born through my mother's screams
which have shadowed me ever since
I freed myself from her womb.

They were her uninterrupted song
singing disdain for my tender wings.

The light inside me reached
to birth into its own sound.

The power inside me needed
to feel the sensation of rising.

The deep heart inside me needed
to know oneness.

The intelligence inside me needed
to sit and ponder this wild world.

My journey to the self
kept my mother's screams in the wind.

DISCERNMENT

I have been hated
but I will not hate.

I have been envied
but I will not envy.

I have been unloved
but I have loved more.

I have been without
but I will not act poor.

I have been condemned
but I will not condemn.

I have not been celebrated
but I will celebrate.

I have been discriminated against
but I will not discriminate.

I have been robbed
but I will not steal.

If you don't have your own philosophy,
do you see what you can become?

TWO WOMEN

She leaned against the Crone tree
Just two old women revealing wrinkled skin
looking forward to morning
when they will share a new day
to the call of the birds.

LEAVES CLAPPING

"Wind, why do you push the leaves so fiercely?" asked the sky. "Why not leave them alone? Aren't they falling fast enough now that summer is ending?"

"Don't you know?" asked the wind. "They asked for help to continue their persistent praise of God. I am helping them fill the air with hallelujahs."

PREVIOUSLY PUBLISHED

"Old Crone." 2nd place winner of Story Circle Poetry Contest published on StoryCircle.org and in *Story Circle Journal Vol. 25 No 4, Dec. 2021.*

ABOUT THE AUTHOR

Jan Marquart is a licensed clinical social worker, educator, author, writing instructor, and motivational speaker.

She has been published in newspapers in New Mexico and California. She has received the National Self-Published Book Award for 2000 from *Writers Digest* for her memoir, *The Breath of Dawn, A Journey of Everyday Blessings*, and received the Editor's Choice Award from the International Library of Poetry for her poem, "Yesterday." In 2013, she won the Editor's Choice award from Story Circle Network for *The Mindful Writer, Still the Mind, Free the Pen*. In 2021 her poem, "Old Crone", won 2nd place in a Story Circle Network international poetry contest.

Most writers have a niche in which they write. Jan enjoys dipping her pen into all genres. Her muse is constantly dancing to different tunes, practicing different structures, and finding her voice in all of them. She has taught writing classes for Life Learning Institute, an organization whose classes focus on those over 50, and Story Circle Network, an international women's writing circle.

Jan's poems, essays, stories, and creative non-fiction pieces have been published online at: www.everywritersresource.com, Poetry Victims, LadyInkMagazine.com, Solecisms, IndianaVoiceJournal.com, Scars Publications (Down in the Dirt), and others.

Blogs: FreeThePen.wordpress.com, AwareLivingNow.blogspot.com

Find all Jan's books at: JanMarquartBooks.com

Email Jan at: jan_marquart@yahoo.com

*9 781732 498396 *